To my grandchildren, Tyce, Trevy,
and Jayla,
  This book was written by a good
friend at our church about her
grand child. We thought you'd like
to read it. Grandma and Grandpa O.

What's Nummy Nadia?

ISBN 978-1-64299-959-4 (paperback)
ISBN 978-1-64349-133-2 (hardcover)
ISBN 978-1-64299-960-0 (digital)

Christian Faith Publishing, Inc.
832 Park Avenue
Meadville, PA 16335
www.christianfaithpublishing.com

Printed in the United States of America

What's Nummy Nadia?

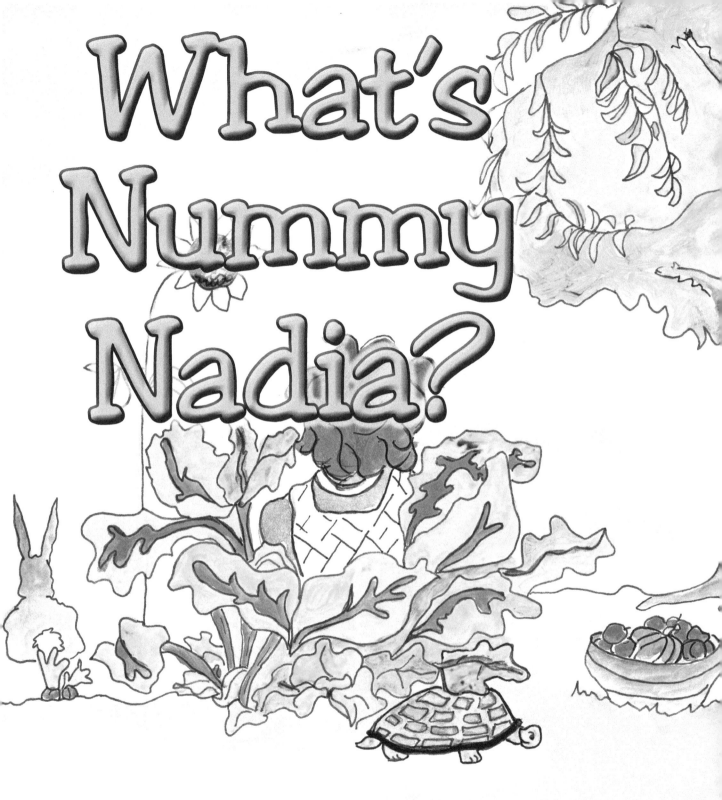

Karen Spicer-Wolven

1

Just before St. Patrick's Day a few years ago, my very first grandbaby was born. She was the most beautiful, tiny baby girl child. I know that all grandmas say that about their grandchildren, but I think that she was gorgeous for certain. Her mommy and daddy named her Nadia.

When Nadia was a few months old, she and her parents moved to sunny Florida to start their own small farm. As her grandma, I would miss her very much. Florida is a long way away from Missouri. That's where I live.

The house that Nadia moved to had enough land that her mommy could grow lots of food for them. She had to start their vegetable garden from scratch. Nadia's mommy was a very good farmer, and she wanted only the healthiest food for little Nadia to eat. *Nummy, nummy* Nadia!

Behind Nadia's new home there were already fruit and nut trees growing. They also had grapevines with big, juicy grapes hanging from them. There were enough grapes for them to make, jams and jellies for their toast. And they had lots of pecans for baking pies for Thanksgiving. *Nummy, nummy* Nadia!

Before she could walk, Nadia's daddy would put her on his shoulders to help pick grapes. Very often, she would squish them in her tiny hands! Her little fingers would turn purple and sticky. *Nummy, nummy* Nadia!

One day, some strange boxes showed up in their backyard. They were beehives! Nadia was still too little to be allowed near them, but her parents had brought them to their farm to pollenate their plants and trees. And, of course, to make honey! *Nummy, nummy* Nadia!

When Nadia was old enough to begin trying different foods, we all started noticing something strange about her favorites. They were all orange! Not everything she liked was the color orange, but most of it! She would eat carrots, sweet potatoes, kumquats, and oranges.

These are all healthy things to eat, but her very favorite meal was mac and cheese. A little mac and cheese is great, but sometimes that's all Nadia would want. *Nummy, nummy* Nadia!

When she would visit her Aunt Teresa, we discovered how much Nadia loved goldfish crackers and Cheetos! Aunt Teresa would keep lots of goldfish at her house, and when I visited, I would bring some too. Grandmas have to be able to spoil their grandchildren. *Nummy, nummy* Nadia!

So Nadia continued to grow, and her mamma planted lots of fruits and vegetables. The rest of us worried that Nadia would not choose to eat green vegetables or fruits that weren't orange, but her mamma knew better. She had more patience than we did. She and Nadia's daddy tried to teach her all about growing and enjoying all kinds of food. *Nummy, nummy* Nadia!

Nadia's mommy and daddy would send pictures of her to me so grandma could see how fast she was growing. I couldn't go to Florida very often to visit, so this was especially important to me.

Nadia's daddy had told me that they were also raising chickens on their little farm. At first, Nadia was afraid of the chickens just like I used to be. Then the next thing I knew, they sent me a picture of Nadia and her chickens asleep in her bedroom together in her play tent! She would also help gather eggs with her mamma. *Nummy, nummy* Nadia!

When I visited Aunt Teresa in the summertime, everybody came over for a big dinner. Nadia's Aunt Jessica and Cousin Jaymes, Grandpa Chris, Uncle Sam, Uncle Jerry, and her mommy and daddy all ate supper together. Aunt Teresa said that we'd better make lots of mac and cheese for Nadia, so we did.

She ate three helpings of mac and cheese but also had some green beans. Later, I caught her with a handful of cashew nuts out of Uncle Jerry's bowl on the coffee table. *Nummy, nummy* Nadia!

29

Nadia's mamma sent me a picture of Nadia that she called "Chomp, Chomp!" Apparently, her mamma had planted swiss chard in pots outside their front door that kept getting chomped on by something.

She thought that it might be rabbits or turtles chewing on it. Then she caught the garden critter in the act. There was Nadia chomping on the swiss chard! *Nummy, nummy Nadia!*

Nadia's mommy soon had lots of plants and food from their farm. So much that they could share with their neighbors and sell their produce and even flowers at the local farmers market. Nadia would go with her mamma to the market.

Her mommy had to keep a close eye on her though, or she would snack on the berries when no one was looking! *Nummy, nummy* Nadia!

Every time that I got pictures of Nadia, she would be doing something new. She was always carrying her chickens around in her arms. Her mamma would show her helping to prepare whatever they had just harvested off their farm.

Nadia was learning how to grow her own food and make delicious meals and treats from her own backyard. This is pretty cool since Nadia is just three years old! *Nummy, nummy* Nadia!

So, really, we shouldn't have worried about Nadia's orange-eating habits. Her parents have taught her to try all sorts of healthy foods. So now, she likes many different foods of all colors. She even knows how to grow them and prepare them lots of ways.

At home, she is surrounded by gardens with flowers, vegetables, fruits, and herbs. She has orchards and pecan groves to run around in. Bees are buzzing happily around while Nadia plays with her chicken friends. It is just the life any grandma wants for her granddaughter.

45

That doesn't mean that Nadia has given up her mac and cheese, Cheetos, and goldfish crackers. She just likes a lot of other stuff now! *Nummy, nummy* Nadia!

About the Author

Karen Spicer-Wolven lives slightly off the beaten path in the Ozark Mountains of Missouri. She lives with her husband Chris, her stepson Sam, and their pit bull Harley in a cabin built of logs reclaimed from downed trees after a tornado found its way through years ago. Her mother-in-law Cathy lives in an adjoining cabin and has been an inspiration to Karen both as a woman of faith and as a writer. Karen grew up in this area with her parents John and Sharon, her twin Teresa, and younger sister Denise. Karen has been blessed to be the mother of four biological children, Ryan, Bethany, Joseph, and Steven and as a grandmother to Nadia, who gives her grandma an excuse to remain forever childlike. She has also had the privilege to be "mom" to her stepchildren, her foster kids, and several kids that just needed a safe place to be for a time. Karen's passions are many and include art, writing, photography, history, and advocating for those not able to do it for themselves. She loves to travel and photograph wildlife, especially orcas, whenever possible. Karen considers the resident orca J, K, and L pods of the San Juan Islands in Washington part of her family as well. Karen is a member of Orange Cumberland Presbyterian Church where she is surrounded by her extended church family and lots of love. Her greatest mission in life is that others see the love of Christ in her and that her life reflects the love that she has been blessed with.